This Journal Belongs To:

Printed in Germany
by Amazon Distribution
GmbH, Leipzig

30579759R00073